My First Romanian
Words for Communication

Picture Book with English Translations

Published By: AuthorUnlock.com

noroc

Cheers

intră

Come In

felicităři

Congratulations

accidentul

Crash

pericol

Danger

foc

Fire

mâncarea

Food

la revedere

Goodbye

la mulţi ani

Happy Birthday

bună ziua

Hello

ajutor

Help

câţi?

How Many?

stânga

Left

hai

Let's go

poate

Maybe

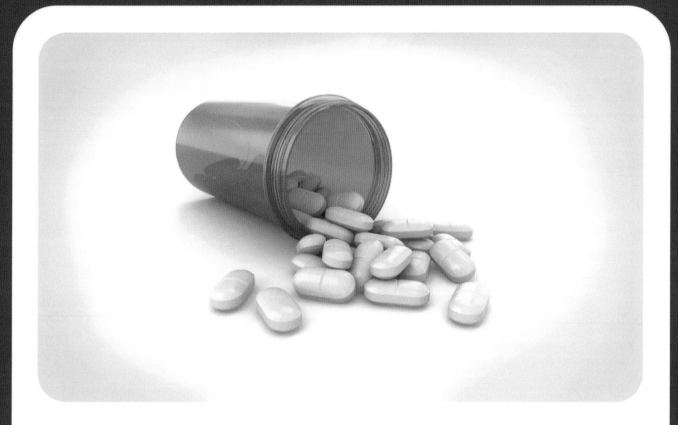

medicamente

Medicine

nu

No

nimic

Nothing

vă rog

Please

trage

Pull

împinge

Push

dreapta

Right

mai încet

Slow Down

curând

Soon

scuze

Sorry

opreşte

Stop

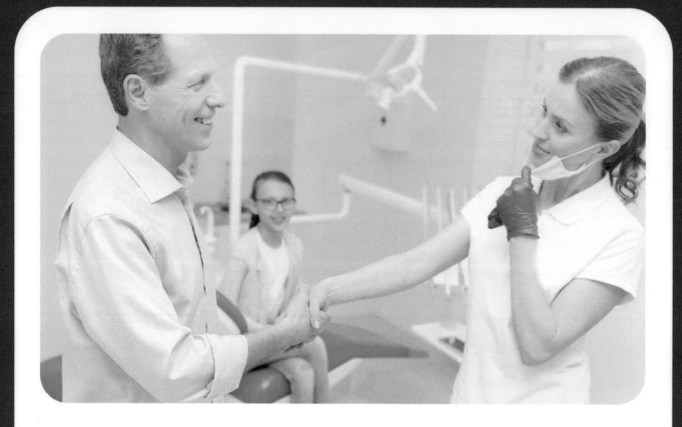

mulțumesc

Thank You

hoţul

Thief

stai

Wait

apa

Water

ce?

What?

când?

When?

unde?

Where?

cine?

Who?

de ce?

Why?

da

Yes